Artificial Intelligence in Pet Care

Solutions for Pets and Their Owners

Table of Contents

1. Introduction 1

2. Understanding AI in Pet Care 2

    2.1. Artificial Intelligence: Unplugged 2

    2.2. AI and The Pet Care Revolution 2

    2.3. Health Monitoring and AI 3

    2.4. Behavioral Understanding with AI 3

    2.5. Challenges and Future Prospects 4

3. Exploring the World of Smart Pet Monitors 6

    3.1. The Rise of Smart Pet Monitors 6

    3.2. Understanding the Key Features 6

    3.3. Examining the Benefits 7

    3.4. Exploring the Next Generation of Pet Monitors 8

4. Unveiling AI-Enhanced Feeding Solutions 10

    4.1. AI-Powered Food Dispensers – Enhancing Portion Control and Diet Monitoring 10

    4.2. Pet Feeders with Facial Recognition 11

    4.3. AI-Apps Interfacing with Smart Feeding Solutions 11

    4.4. The Drive towards Smart Feeding Bowls 12

    4.5. Customized Feeding based on Activity Level 12

    4.6. The Horizon: What's Next for AI in Pet Feeding 13

5. Interpreting Emotions: Pet Behavior Analysis via AI 14

    5.1. The Landscape of Emotion Interpretation 14

    5.2. Decoding Emotions: AI Algorithms 15

    5.3. Smart Devices for Pet-Owners 15

    5.4. The Impact on Pet Health and Behavior 16

    5.5. The Challenges and Avenues for Future Development 16

6. Proactive Pet Health Tracking: AI at Work 18

    6.1. Evolving Pet Care — A Technological Revolution 18

6.2. Wearable Tech — Continuous Monitoring, Real-time Data . . . 19

6.3. Smart Feeders — An Intelligent Diet Supervisor 19

6.4. AI-Powered Mobile Apps — Holistic Pet Care at Your
Fingertips 20

6.5. Harnessing AI for Predictive Pet Health Insights 20

6.6. Enriching The Bond — Emotional Wellness Meets Tech 21

7. The Future of Veterinary Assistance: AI-Based Innovations 22

7.1. The Intersection of AI and Pet Health Care 22

7.2. Embracing Vet-tech: AI tools for Veterinarians 23

7.3. Vet Chatbots: AI-managed Pet Health 24

7.4. Predictive Analysis and Health Monitoring 24

7.5. Conclusion: A New Dawn for Pet Health Care 25

8. AI & Your Pet: The Ethical Considerations 26

8.1. Understanding The Ethics of AI in Pet Care 26

8.2. Unpacking the Animal Autonomy Factor 27

8.3. Navigating the Opaque Realm of Pet Privacy 27

8.4. AI Accountability and Liability 28

8.5. Bridging the Affective Computing Gap 28

9. Transforming Pet Training with AI 30

9.1. The Advent of AI in Pet Training 30

9.2. How AI Works in Pet Training 30

9.3. AI-powered Pet Training Gadgets 31

9.4. The Intersection of AI and Interactive Plays 32

9.5. Closing Thoughts 32

10. AI and Exotic Pets: A New Frontier 34

10.1. AI-Assisted Habitat Simulation 34

10.2. Dietary Management 35

10.3. Health Monitoring Systems 35

10.4. AI Applications in Exotic Pet Training 36

10.5. Ethical Concerns and Regulatory Matters 36

11. What's Next? Predicting the Future of AI in Pet Care 38

11.1. Predictive Analytics, Health Tracking, and AI-Driven
Veterinarians 38

11.2. AI and Nutrition Management 39

11.3. Computer Vision for Behavior Analysis 39

11.4. Automated and Enhanced Training through AI 40

11.5. Robotics and AI Interaction 41

Chapter 1. Introduction

In this Special Report, we plunge into an exciting convergence of technology and pet care - "Artificial Intelligence in Pet Care: Solutions for Pets and Their Owners." Offering a friendly, digestible navigation through this innovative domain, we seek to unwrap the revolutionary ways tech is reshaping the pet care industry. This report elaborates on the remarkable application of AI solutions, from smart pet monitors to proactive health tracking tools, radically enhancing the lives of our precious animals and their devoted owners. If you're a pet lover eager to discover the latest trends and advancements enriching the quality of pet-ownership, this report paves the way to a future where you can connect with your pets like never before. Dive into the splendid world of enhanced pet care, interlaced with technology, and prepare to embrace a lifestyle that's both pet-friendly and futuristic - because understanding isn't simply for humans!

Chapter 2. Understanding AI in Pet Care

Artificial Intelligence (AI) has increasingly found its way into many industries, revolutionizing the way we live, work, play, and, particularly, how we care for our pets. Understanding how AI works in pet care is crucial to appreciate this transformative technology fully. By shedding light on how AI is transforming pet care, we take you on a journey through the nuts and bolts of this remarkable convergence.

2.1. Artificial Intelligence: Unplugged

Artificial Intelligence refers to a wide-ranging branch of computer science responsible for building intelligent machines capable of performing tasks that typically require human intelligence. These tasks may encompass learning from experience, recognizing patterns, understanding language, sensing and perceiving the environment, or making decisions. A defining feature of AI is that it's not merely programmed to execute a set task; it learns, adapts, and improves over time.

2.2. AI and The Pet Care Revolution

Complex AI systems are now being harnessed to serve our furry friends in ways that had been mere fantasy a few years ago. The pet care industry today deploys AI technology to provide significant enhancements to the quality of life for pets, while easing the challenges of pet ownership.

Automated feeders now use AI to regulate feeding schedules and manage dietary requirements based on an individual pet's breed, age, weight, and activity level. AI-powered cameras deliver real-time updates on pets' behaviors, notifying owners if something seems amiss. Smart pet doors use AI to recognize and permit entry only to pets, keeping unwelcome animals outside.

In essence, AI's reach in the pet care industry traverses dimensions from routine tasks like feeding and entry control to more complex areas like health monitoring and behavior analysis.

2.3. Health Monitoring and AI

Arguably one of AI's most profound impacts in pet care is in the realm of health monitoring. Advanced health monitoring tools infused with AI capabilities are providing groundbreaking solutions in monitoring and managing our pets' wellbeing.

AI-powered pet wearables, such as smart collars, can monitor heart rate, respiration, sleep patterns, and overall activity levels. Any irregularities trigger alerts to pet owners on their smartphones. These real-time notifications can often make a critical difference, allowing for immediate veterinary intervention and potentially preventing escalated health issues.

AI systems also assist veterinarians in diagnosing complex conditions with greater accuracy. Machine learning models, a subset of AI, can be trained on vast datasets of pet medical records to accurately identify hard-to-detect diseases, ensuring early treatment and increased chances of recovery.

2.4. Behavioral Understanding with AI

AI lends itself as a powerful tool in understanding and interpreting your pet's behavior. It accomplishes this by enabling devices to learn ongoing patterns and make sense of them over time.

For instance, AI-powered pet cameras observe pets' behavior, learn from it, and then provide insights to pet owners. If your dog spends excessive time near the window, the AI could infer anxiety or boredom and advise on behavioral modification strategies.

Likewise, AI in pet toys takes engagement to a new level. These toys can mimic the pet's play style, keep them mentally stimulated, and reduce destructive behavior due to boredom.

The intersection of AI and pet care also aids in pet training. AI-powered tools can generate behavior reports, helping owners and professional trainers understand the patterns and devise effective training methods.

2.5. Challenges and Future Prospects

While AI holds incredible potential in revolutionizing pet care, it is not without its challenges. Data privacy and the potential for AI to form inaccurate findings stand out. However, advancements in AI research and development promise to iron out these kinks, instilling more confidence in the systems.

Unleashing AI's potential in pet care could spell a future where smart homes integrate pet care routines, vets use AI to provide personalized treatment plans, and we unravel more about our pets' behaviors and health needs.

In conclusion, AI in pet care is more than just a luxury or novelty - it's a growing trend that eases the lives of pets and owners alike, offering a glimpse into the future of pet ownership. Understanding how AI contributes to pet care allows us to appreciate not only the innovation but also the enhanced companionship it brings. While there is much terrain to explore and many challenges to conquer, AI's potential in pet care is immense and full of exciting prospects.

Chapter 3. Exploring the World of Smart Pet Monitors

Imagine a world where you can keep an eye on your cats or dogs even when you're away, a world where you can monitor, guide, and cater to your pets' needs remotely. Welcome to the future of pet care – the world of Smart Pet Monitors. Powered by advanced A.I. technology, these devices open new vistas of interface between pets and pet parents, transcending the boundaries of physical presence and geographical restrictions.

3.1. The Rise of Smart Pet Monitors

With the dawn of the digital era, pet care has also undergone significant evolution. Traditional means of looking after pets – relying on neighbors or hiring a pet sitter – are now supplemented and often surpassed by the advent of smart pet monitors. These devices, connected via the internet and equipped with A.I. technology, allow pet owners to keep constant vigilance on their pets, irrespective of where they are physically.

These technologies have proven to be a game-changer for pet parents who lead busy lives and for pets that need constant supervision. Elderly animals, pets with medical conditions, or even the more mischievous ones can now be cared for without interruptions. With video and audio capabilities, treat dispensers, and even interactive functionality, smart pet monitors have indeed reshaped pet care, creating a harmonious balance between human routines and pets' wellbeing.

3.2. Understanding the Key Features

Smart pet monitors come with a plethora of features, all aimed at solving the unique challenges of pet-care. Let us delve into some of the most significant features that genuinely make these devices 'smart.'

1. *Remote Video Monitoring*: This allows pet owners to visually monitor their pets anytime, from anywhere. Equipped with high-definition cameras, these devices provide a live feed, allowing owners to track their pets' activities.

2. *Two-Way Audio*: With built-in speakers and microphones, these devices offer two-way communication between owners and their pets. This is particularly useful for pets suffering from separation anxiety.

3. *Treat Dispensers*: Many models come with this interactive feature. At the touch of a button, owners can dispense their pets' favorite treats remotely, rewarding good behavior or pacifying distressed pets.

4. *Motion and Sound Alerts*: Powered by intelligent machine learning algorithms, these devices can recognize unusual patterns based on motion or sound and alert the pet owner instantly.

5. *Night Vision*: The built-in infrared technology allows owners to keep an eye on their pets even in the dark.

3.3. Examining the Benefits

Integrated with powerful A.I. technologies, Smart Pet Monitors offer an array of benefits that enhance the quality of life for both pets and their owners.

1. *Peace of Mind*: The biggest advantage of smart pet monitors lies in providing peace of mind to the pet owners. Whether you're at work, on vacation, or just out for an errand, you no longer need to worry about your pet's wellbeing.

2. *Reduced Separation Anxiety*: Through two-way communication, pets can hear their owner's voice, significantly easing their separation anxiety.

3. *Better Understanding of Pets' Behaviour*: Constant monitoring can help owners understand their pets' behavior better, aiding in early detection of any changes indicating potential health issues, changes in mood, or alterations in routine.

4. *Increased Interaction*: Interactive features like treat dispensers not only help in training but also allow for meaningful interaction, strengthening the bond between pets and their owners.

3.4. Exploring the Next Generation of Pet Monitors

The evolution of smart pet monitors isn't stopping here. Futuristic models are currently in the pipeline, equipped with advanced features like facial recognition, heartbeat monitoring, A.I.-enabled health trackers, and more.

Imagine a world where your pet monitor could identify different pets based on facial recognition, dispense individual treats, and even monitor vital signs to pre-empt potential health issues. Or, think of a scenario where health alerts could be integrated with local veterinary services for immediate response in case of emergency. The future of smart pet monitors is rife with possibilities, providing a vista towards a world where pets' care embraces technology like never before.

Smart Pet Monitors have revolutionized our relationship with our pets, taking it beyond the confines of physical proximity and ushering in an era where our care, affection, and responsibility transcend geographical locations and time-zones. As we continue to explore how technology is transforming pet care, one thing is certain:

The bond between pets and their owners is set to deepen further, powered by these incredible advancements in AI technology.

Chapter 4. Unveiling AI-Enhanced Feeding Solutions

In the domain of pet care, one of the significant aspects where AI and technology have made revolutionary changes is feeding solutions. The blend of artificial intelligence with pet feeding mechanisms has helped introduce exciting innovations at the intersection of pet health and convenience for pet owners. This chapter explores various AI-enhanced feeding solutions that have dramatically advanced pet care standards.

4.1. AI-Powered Food Dispensers – Enhancing Portion Control and Diet Monitoring

The core of AI-based feeding solutions rests on the automated food dispensers equipped with artificial intelligence. These innovative solutions are designed to regulate the diet of pets, precisely controlling portions and tracking the amount of food consumed. They help pet owners schedule meals, ensure portion control, and maintain dietary consistency – effectively preventing obesity and other dietary-related health conditions in pets.

AI-powered food dispensers come with integrated databases that can recognize a variety of pet food types. By assessing the nutritional content in the selected pet food, they can recommend the ideal portion size for your pet based on its specific needs including breed, age, weight, and activity level.

Smart dispensers can also help identify if a pet is not eating as much as they usually do, a possible early sign of a health issue. This crucial information can alert pet owners and veterinarians, promoting early diagnosis and intervention.

4.2. Pet Feeders with Facial Recognition

In multi-pet households, ensuring that each pet gets the appropriate food and portion can be incredibly challenging. To tackle this tricky issue, innovators have introduced pet feeders with facial recognition technology.

Utilizing advanced AI algorithms, these smart feeders can identify pets based on unique facial characteristics, allowing for specific dietary routines for each pet in the household. They can dispense specific types and amounts of food based on the identified pet, ensuring each receives the right nutrition. No longer will your larger pet steal the smaller one's food!

This development distinguishes pets based on their dietary needs, helps maintain a balanced diet for each pet, and significantly reduces the potential of overeating, food aggression, and food theft.

4.3. AI-Apps Interfacing with Smart Feeding Solutions

If pet owners are away from their homes during meal times, they need not worry. Several AI-enhanced feeding solutions come with compatible mobile applications, enabling owners to feed their pets remotely.

Through these applications, pet owners can monitor their pet's eating patterns in real-time, receive alerts on their eating habits, and manually adjust feeding times and portions. These apps also record feeding data for future reference, helping pet owners and vets make informed decisions about diet adjustments.

4.4. The Drive towards Smart Feeding Bowls

Entering into the realm of advanced functionality, we find smart feeding bowls equipped with weight sensing technology. These AI-infused feeding devices can accurately measure the weight of the food given to pets, helping pet owners provide precise feed portions matched to their pet's dietary needs.

Technologies like radio-frequency identification (RFID) are also employed in some smart bowls to identify the pet intending to eat. This function helps prevent a pet from eating another's food, helping to keep a multi-pet household's feeding in harmony.

4.5. Customized Feeding based on Activity Level

As we continue stitching AI into our everyday lives, we're now seeing a transformative idea – personalized pet feeding schedules based on a pet's activity level. By syncing smart activity monitors with AI-equipped feeders, feeding solutions can now adjust food portions and schedules based on how active a pet has been during the day.

For an active dog who enjoys a long morning walk, for instance, their AI-enhanced feeder can ensure that they receive a proportionate amount of calories for the exercise they've performed. In contrast, for a lazy day with less activity, their portion could decrease automatically to avoid overeating.

This level of customized feeding keeps pets healthy and prevents obesity and other health problems that can arise from overfeeding or underfeeding.

4.6. The Horizon: What's Next for AI in Pet Feeding

The surface of what AI can bring to the pet care industry, especially in feeding solutions, has merely been scratched. The evolution of AI technology and its convergence with IoT and wearable technology would usher in possibilities like health monitoring feeding bowls, or feeders dispensing food based on real-time health data.

In conclusion, AI-enhanced feeding solutions signify a bright future, creating new paradigms of care for our pets. They ensure a healthier and happier lifestyle for pets and offer pet owners peace of mind that their loved ones are receiving the best in care, convenience, and nutrition. The future will undoubtedly reveal even more astounding breakthroughs in this enthralling intersection of technology and pet care. Embracing these futuristic solutions is not just a choice, but an exciting journey towards an enriched pet-parenting experience.

It's high time we reimagined the way we feed our pets - and with AI, we're off to an impressive start. The next era of pet care is here, and it's powered by artificial intelligence.

Chapter 5. Interpreting Emotions: Pet Behavior Analysis via AI

One of the revolutionary utilities of artificial intelligence in pet care is in the sphere of emotion interpretation and behavior analysis. Researchers and tech developers worldwide fuse data analytics and deep learning algorithms to decode and understand our pets' emotions and behaviors. With this, we can further empathize with our furry friends, respond better to their needs, and drive towards a more fruitful coexistence.

5.1. The Landscape of Emotion Interpretation

Emotion interpretation in pets, although in the nascent stages, is fast gaining popularity. Predominantly, the foundation lies in recognizing that pets, just like human beings, exhibit a wide range of emotions. From happiness and excitement to fear and anxiety, our pets often rely on non-verbal communication, exhibiting key behavioral signs. This forms the pivotal point for AI-powered tools, which aim to analyze these behaviors, interpret their meanings, and provide insightful feedback to pet owners.

Conversely, misinterpretation of an animal's emotion can lead to an array of problems, namely stress, behavioral issues, or even health problems. Hence, there is increasing impetus on ensuring accurate emotion interpretation, which is where AI technology comes into play.

5.2. Decoding Emotions: AI Algorithms

Artificial Intelligence assists in interlacing the pieces of emotion interpretation. It starts with identifying typical behaviors that pets exhibit and mapping these with certain emotions. For instance, certain movements or actions of a pet may correspond to excitement or anxiety. AI uses extensive datasets, deep learning algorithms, and intense photographic or video analysis to make these correlations. The more data it trains with, the better it becomes at predicting the emotion behind a particular behavior.

The algorithms function by segmenting the creature's movements into individual 'key points', which can be indicative of a particular mood or emotion. Then, using a technique named 'pose estimation,' these key points are compared against a database of countless other pet behaviors, allowing the AI tool to recognize patterns and predict the pet's emotional state.

5.3. Smart Devices for Pet-Owners

Given its promising scope, there are a number of AI-powered tools developed for pet owners. One such example is smart cameras, which continuously monitor pets in their natural habitats. They capture typical behaviors and transmit the data to a cloud database. From there, AI algorithms analyze these behaviors, make correlations, and provide insights on the probable emotions the pet might be experiencing.

To make the system more user-friendly, these insights are typically sent through mobile app notifications. Thus, pet owners can keep a check on their pets instantaneously and from anywhere, not bound by proximity.

5.4. The Impact on Pet Health and Behavior

The application of AI in interpreting pet emotions has substantial implications for the health and behavior of pets. Spotting signs of distress, anxiety, or discomfort earlier can lead to timely veterinary intervention, potentially preventing more severe health issues. For instance, cats often hide their discomfort, and deciphering their subtle cues may help alert owners to possible health issues. This aspect of proactive care, enabled by AI, can transform pet healthcare as we know it.

Moreover, understanding the pets' emotions can assist pet parents in managing their behaviour. By accurately interpreting their pets' emotions, they can interact more effectively, reducing stress or anxiety and averting behavioral issues. This unravels a new realm of how we relate with our furry friends, enabling deeper bonds and mutual understanding.

5.5. The Challenges and Avenues for Future Development

Despite promising advancements, there are areas where the use of AI for emotion interpretation stands challenged. The individual variations among animals of the same species can pose significant impediments to creating standardized algorithms that could apply to a majority of pets. Moreover, a misinterpretation by the AI could have serious repercussions on a pet's welfare.

On the bright side, the evolution of AI, paired with ongoing research on animal behavior and emotions, promises exciting and innovative developments for the future. Further study and refinement in machine learning algorithms and predictive analytics could lead to sophisticated AI tools capable of deciphering the most subtle nuances of pet emotions.

Artificial Intelligence in emotional and behavioral interpretation for pets is a burgeoning area with bountiful opportunities for growth, exploration, and improvement. The adoption of these technologies offers pet owners unprecedented insights into their pets' minds, fostering a better understanding and connection. While certain challenges need to be addressed, innovations in the field promise a future where we can understand the language of our pets - as understanding isn't simply for humans!

Chapter 6. Proactive Pet Health Tracking: AI at Work

The twenty-first century has seen a dramatic shift from the traditional reactive approach to pet care towards a proactive strategy, heavily powered by artificial intelligence. Recognizing irregular patterns, predicting potential health threats, and ensuring the overall well-being of pets is at the heart of this transformative journey. With intricate algorithms, sophisticated sensors, and AI-driven apps, pet owners can now maintain a vigilant eye and a comforting hand on the health of their furry companions.

6.1. Evolving Pet Care — A Technological Revolution

Pet care has transformed remarkably over the years, evolving beyond scheduled veterinary visits and random health check-ups. Today, it stands driven by technology. The integration of AI isn't a mere 'bells and whistles' addition to the pet care industry - it's a game-changing revolution that empowers pet owners with unprecedented tools to monitor and manage their pet's health.

In the era of digitization and immediate information, pet owners seek continuous insights into their pet's health, striving to provide optimal care. AI bridges that critical gap by offering an intelligent, personal, and responsive health tracking mechanism. Wearable tech, smart pet feeders, AI-powered mobile apps, among other advancements, work as an ensemble to interpret pet behavior, identify health issues, and provide actionable insights.

6.2. Wearable Tech — Continuous Monitoring, Real-time Data

A pioneering advancement in proactive pet health care are AI-enabled wearables. They're designed to perform different roles - from tracking exercise levels to analyzing sleep patterns, these sensors have positioned themselves as first-rate preventive healthcare tools.

However, these devices aren't just miniature versions of human-centric wearables – they vault over the challenges of monitoring a creature who can neither report symptoms nor express problems. By deciphering subtle patterns in body temperature, heart rate, breathing rate, and sleep, this AI-powered gear distills loads of data into digestible insights for the owners. Moreover, integrating with smartphones, they offer real-time updates on pets' health, ensuring immediate response when abnormalities are observed.

6.3. Smart Feeders — An Intelligent Diet Supervisor

Next in the line of AI arsenal are smart pet feeders, an innovation that strictly manages pets' nutritional needs. With AI's ability to learn from the past and predict optimal feeding schedules, pet owners can tailor diets according to their pets' health requirements and habits.

Smart feeders can dramatically reduce cases of underfeeding or overfeeding, largely preventing related disorders. They can also work in sync with wearable devices, adjusting food portions and meal times based on real-time activity data of the pet. This integration forms a cohesive AI-driven mechanism for managing pets' nutrition and overall health proactively.

6.4. AI-Powered Mobile Apps — Holistic Pet Care at Your Fingertips

The entrance of AI in the mobile app sphere has further boosted accessibility and convenience in proactive pet health management. AI-powered apps can interpret and track animals' behavioral patterns, vocal signals, and physical condition, providing a holistic health overview.

Some apps leverage image recognition algorithms to detect potential health issues visible on the pets' skin or fur. Others utilize AI to interpret animal sounds, identifying signs of distress or illness. The built-in databases hold extensive knowledge about various animal diseases and conditions, which gets constantly updated, further enabling accurate diagnosis and proactive care.

6.5. Harnessing AI for Predictive Pet Health Insights

AI's greatest strength lies in its ability to harness data intelligently. With machine learning models, it can analyze vast amounts of data, anticipate patterns, and predict potential health complications. It allows pet owners to pivot from a reactive approach towards a more preventive methodology, leading to early detection and diagnosis.

For instance, the AI's ability to discern minute changes in fur patterns and skin conditions could suggest an early stage skin allergy, initiating prompt intervention. Similarly, an irregularity in sleep patterns may hint at underlying disorders. Here, AI facilitates the recognition of health threats well before they escalate, drastically reducing complexities and costs associated with late-stage treatment.

6.6. Enriching The Bond — Emotional Wellness Meets Tech

While physical health is an integral component, emotional wellness of pets can't be overlooked. Here again, AI is taking enormous strides. By interpreting animals' behaviors, sounds, and expressions, AI can help identify and alleviate stressors affecting pets. This promotes a positive and enriching environment for pets, nurturing the human-animal bond.

AI technology is indeed transforming the pet care domain, enhancing the lives of pets and their owners. With proactive measures becoming the new norm, reactive methods are gradually shifting to the background. This advanced, technology-laced pet care sector brings about a future where understanding isn't simply for humans. And as our AI tools continue to learn and grow, so will the quality of the care we provide for our beloved pets, ensuring that their health, happiness, and wellness stay forever in focus.

Chapter 7. The Future of Veterinary Assistance: AI-Based Innovations

The advent of technology has been at the helm of transforming various industries. The veterinary field is no exception, with the introduction of artificial intelligence (AI) radically altering the conventional facets of pet care. A dramatically evolving field, AI in veterinary assistance endeavors to redefine both the nature of care delivered and the way it is executed.

7.1. The Intersection of AI and Pet Health Care

At this juncture, it's essential to gain an insight into the overlapping of AI with pet health care and the potency this union brings forth. Artificial intelligence essentially formulates systems capable of mimicking human intelligence, endeavoring to intrigue and resolve complex scenarios. In the pet health context, this ability goes beyond robotic process automation to offer solutions that include predictive analytics, machine vision, natural language processing, and much more.

In the pet health arena, the fusion of AI is an attempt to navigate the challenges of capturing pet behaviors, understanding symptoms, and diagnosing health conditions, simplifying the entire process for both the vets and pet owners.

An instance of AI implementation in pet health care is machine learning algorithms that analyze the behavior of pets to anticipate potential health issues. For instance, recognizing abnormalities in a pet's eating, sleeping, or physical activity patterns can signify potential health complications. AI tools can help detect these early signs, enabling proactive measures to support pet health.

AI has the ability to augment the scope of veterinary assistance, pushing the envelope on problem-solving and decision-making in pet health care. From simplifying diagnostics to enhancing patient service, AI promises to be a significant game changer.

7.2. Embracing Vet-tech: AI tools for Veterinarians

Artificial intelligence's incursions into the medical field are not novel. Be it predicting diseases, assisting surgeries, or simplifying data management, AI has been an incredible accomplice in human health care. Applying similar concepts to veterinary medicine, one can envision the revolutionary shift this can instigate.

AI-powered tools can help veterinarians sift through vast amounts of data in record time, thereby facilitating quick diagnoses and treatment plans. Furthermore, AI solutions can drastically cut down the margin of error in terms of misdiagnoses and treatment, directly improving the quality of pet care.

For example, telehealth services for pets have started to employ AI algorithms that can observe and analyze patterns in pet behavior and vital signs. Veterinarians can access the data remotely, helping them diagnose and treat pets from afar.

Automated machines enabled with robotic process automation can take over the mundane task of managing and updating patient records, schedules, and paperwork, allowing practitioners more room for focusing on actual pet care.

7.3. Vet Chatbots: AI-managed Pet Health

With technology becoming an integral part of our daily lives, it's no surprise that AI-powered chatbots are stepping into the pet health arena. Vet chatbots leverage AI to respond to pet owners' queries, alleviate their concerns, and advise on preventative measures or treatments.

AI-managed vet chatbots mimic the quality of professional consultation, which can be beneficial in scenarios where immediate access to a vet is not feasible. The chatbots, equipped with machine learning and natural language processing, interpret the problems faced by pet owners and provide advice based on a vast database of veterinary medicine and symptom analysis. They understand and respond to nuanced signs of distress in pets and can even guide the owner to take emergency measures if needed.

While these chatbots may not replace actual veterinary consultation, they can provide immediate help, offer basic pet health advice, and facilitate emergency care.

7.4. Predictive Analysis and Health Monitoring

The AI-enabled predictive analysis in pet health care is a growing domain with immense potential. Predictive analytics tools can foretell potential health conditions based on the pet's behavioral data, helping to prevent or manage them effectively.

AI-based health monitoring devices facilitate the collection of vital data points. These devices, often wearable, capture everything from activity levels to heart rates and sleeping patterns. When this real-time data is processed through predictive algorithms, the possibilities are multifold. We can foresee diseases, understand the impacts of medications, and give owners a profound understanding of their pet's health.

Predictive analytics moves the pet health care domain from reactive to proactive, majorly restraining the onset of diseases or severe health conditions, contributing to the quality and longevity of pet health.

7.5. Conclusion: A New Dawn for Pet Health Care

As we embrace the future of veterinary assistance, it's evident that AI-based innovations are just at their inception. With continuous research and advancements, the AI landscape in pet care will continue to enrich and evolve, offering efficient, smart solutions to transform the lives of pets and their caregivers.

These advancements will not only translate to better care and improved quality of life for pets, but they will also support veterinarians in their practice, empowering them to deliver care with increased ease, speed, and effectiveness. AI in veterinary assistance is not just a looming possibility - it's an inevitable reality.

While we revel in these technological advancements, we must remember that AI is an assistant, a tool to enhance our capabilities. It's the human touch, the bond between a pet and their caregiver, that sits at the heart of pet care. AI promises to enhance that bond, making it possible to love and care for our pets in ways we've never imagined before.

Chapter 8. AI & Your Pet: The Ethical Considerations

The exciting convergence of technology and pet care has brought with it a host of revolutionary, practical solutions designed to enrich the lives of pets and their owners alike. These state-of-the-art AI tools, from smart pet monitors to proactive health tracking devices, promise a radical overhaul of pet care, reaching further than ever before. However, amidst this exciting wave of progress, it's critically important to pause and reflect on the ethical implications of incorporating AI into our pets' lives.

8.1. Understanding The Ethics of AI in Pet Care

AI, short for Artificial Intelligence, possesses the ability to learn from and respond to its environment, analyzing patterns and predicting outcomes based on available data. When used in pet care, AI caters to the natural and personalised needs of your pets, often helping to diagnose and prevent health issues. However, the integration of AI in pet care also raises comprehensive ethical considerations. Fundamental among them is the need to ensure humane treatment of our pets. Using AI tools, how far can we go before we overlook the animal's natural behavior, invading their privacy and autonomy?

There's also the issue of responsibility. Should AI tools misinterpret a vital sign resulting in an incorrect diagnosis, who holds accountability - the AI developers or the pet owners relying on their technology?

8.2. Unpacking the Animal Autonomy Factor

AI tools such as smart collars and monitors inevitably affect an animal's environment. These devices, while transformative and practical, may inadvertently disrupt an animal's natural behavior and infringe on their normal course of activities. Often, the pet may not be comfortable with the device, leading to distress or apprehension, which may only be visible to the attentive pet owner.

Such situations demonstrate an urgent need to design AI-tools keeping the animal's autonomy and comfort paramount. Failure to respect the pet's personal space or overriding its natural behavior can lead to prolonged stress, deteriorating health, or altered behavior. The ethical challenge here lies in offering solutions that strike a balance between advanced care and respect for the animal's autonomy.

8.3. Navigating the Opaque Realm of Pet Privacy

Pet monitors and other AI devices often gather and store substantial amounts of personal data, including information about pet behaviour patterns and health conditions. Despite pets' inability to comprehend the implications of privacy, safeguarding of their personal information becomes a non-negotiable ethical imperative.

The information collected by AI must adhere to stringent data management protocols, ensuring data security and privacy. Ensuring pets' privacy goes beyond safeguarding their data from hackers and leaks. It extends to guaranteeing transparency about what data is collected, how it is used, and who has access to it.

8.4. AI Accountability and Liability

Another significant concern is the responsibility of diagnosis and care. Upon incorrect diagnosis or misleading insights, who is to be held accountable? Is it the AI developers, who designed the technology, or the pet owners, who chose to implement it?

These questions underscore the necessity for stringent checks and balances within the AI-powered pet care system. A protocol must exist to share responsibility between developers, users, and possibly, regulatory bodies. This shared responsibility model would not only improve system accountability but also the reliability of AI tools and devices.

8.5. Bridging the Affective Computing Gap

An area of AI that holds immense significance in the pet care industry is affective computing, where AI systems are programmed to recognize, interpret, and respond to pet emotions. This capability, while highly promising, also poses potential risks and ethical considerations.

AI systems designed to understand and meet pet's emotional needs must be as authentic as possible. They must be sensitive to a pet's unique personality and disposition, to mimic an empathetic response. This demands an extraordinary level of transparency, authenticity, and ethical mindfulness in AI design.

Relying heavily on AI-powered tools to interpret and meet pets' emotional requirements can also result in pet owners becoming detached from their pets. Encouraging an over-reliance on technology may inadvertently cause pet owners to miss out on the nuances of pet care, creating a further gap between AI and ethical considerations.

As we stand on the brink of this immense technological evolution, the ethical considerations of AI in pet care cannot be overlooked. The impact of AI solutions extends beyond convenience and practicality - it reaches deep into the lives and welfare of our pets. Therefore, we must ensure that as we leap forward in technological progress, we do so responsibly - with thorough consideration of the ethical implications involved in our choices.

Chapter 9. Transforming Pet Training with AI

Let's start our journey with one of the most surprising interfaces where AI and pet care converse - pet training. As any pet owner would attest, training can be both a rewarding and exhausting aspect of pet ownership. Traditional training methods, while effective, can be time-consuming and require consistency. Enter the revolutionary world of AI, reshaping the landscape of pet training with advanced technologies and sophisticated learning algorithms.

9.1. The Advent of AI in Pet Training

Historically, training pets have relied heavily on human intervention and time investment. Conventional methods are highly dependent on individuals' capabilities to understand animal behaviours and deploy tactics accordingly. The inherent shortcomings of these methods led to the exploration of more sophisticated approaches - cue Artificial Intelligence.

The advent of AI in pet training interfaces a new era of possibilities. Now, Artificial Intelligence isn't just about technology recognizing pet behaviors; it's about responding effectively, eliminating guesswork and reducing miscommunication between pets and their owners. This application of AI provides an optimised, effective, and less laborious approach to training pets.

9.2. How AI Works in Pet Training

The use of AI in pet training, in essence, mimics the "reward and punishment" mechanism used traditionally. However, technology allows for scalability and precision unparalleled by human counterparts. At the heart of pet training with AI are complex algorithms that are programmed to recognize certain behaviors based on a plethora of training data.

AI systems are "trained" by feeding them a massive database of images and video sequences illustrating particular pets' behavior, together with labels - something called supervised learning. Over time, the AI begins to recognize patterns and can accurately label new, unseen behaviors. This gives us AI's potential in pet training: the ability to understand, and react in real-time to a pet's behavior.

9.3. AI-powered Pet Training Gadgets

Several modern pet training gadgets leverage AI's might. These devices utilize compound sensors, cameras, and microphones to capture a pet's actions and sounds comprehensively. For example, pet cameras equipped with AI can discern between different pet behaviors - barking, scratching, pacing - and respond accordingly with pre-programmed stimuli or alerts.

Likewise, AI-powered wearables transform pet training by facilitating monitoring and offering real-time updates. An excellent illustration of such technology is AI-embedded pet collars. Not only do they monitor pets' physical activities, but they can detect stress levels, barks, and other sounds, providing owners insights to adjust training techniques in response.

Bark recognition AI gadgets allow owners to understand and control incessant barking effectively, as these devices differentiate between different types of barking and alert owners. Some advanced models even dispense rewards when the dog remains quiet for a specified duration, assisting in constructive reinforcement conditioning.

9.4. The Intersection of AI and Interactive Plays

AI's transformative touch extends beyond simple behavior correction and reaches experimental fields like interactive play, which offers a unique gamification perspective in pet training.

Companies have begun to develop smart toys that use AI to engage pets in stimulating games based on their individual preferences. These devices don't just entertain pets, they also serve to enforce positive behaviors. For instance, a cat toy that only drops treats when the pet exhibits certain desired behaviors, such as not scratching furniture, instills good habits while keeping them entertained.

9.5. Closing Thoughts

In conclusion, the integration of AI into pet training is a comprehensive and ever-evolving domain. It provides a sculpted enhancement of old training methods and paves the way for effective, less labor-intensive alternatives. With continued advancements, artificial intelligence might pioneer techniques that could transform how we perceive pet training - shaping a future where you can understand your pet better and form a more profound bond. AI is adjusting the pet care industry with tools built not just for simplification, but for a deeper, more rewarding relationship between pets and their owners.

However, it's critical to note the limitations in what AI can truly comprehend. Pets indeed respond to stimuli conditioned by AI, but it's the emotional connection and understanding between pet and owner that ultimately lead to more effective training. Hence, the integration of AI in pet training should ideally work as a supplement to traditional training methods, not an absolute replacement. AI's application in pet training has immense potential, but it's our responsibility as pet owners to use this groundbreaking technology to enhance the nurturing relationship we share with our pets, not bypass it.

Chapter 10. AI and Exotic Pets: A New Frontier

AI technologies, albeit novel, have swiftly navigated the realm of pet care, extending their reach far beyond traditional pets like dogs and cats. They are entering uncharted territory: the care of exotic pets. This chapter will highlight an adventurous journey of AI meeting exotic pet care, illustrating how it is making groundbreaking improvements in this niche. Let's venture into this fascinating convergence, exploring how AI's novelty becomes a game-changer for exotic pet owners and their unique pets.

10.1. AI-Assisted Habitat Simulation

The first concern when dealing with exotic pets is ensuring that their habitats are closely mimicked. From reptiles to tropical birds, exotic pets originate from diverse climates and environments which should be accurately replicated for their optimum health. This task becomes less daunting with the incorporation of AI.

AI-enabled devices, such as smart terrariums or aquariums, have proven beneficial for exotic pet owners. These habitats, parsed with sensors, are capable of monitoring and adjusting the environment's elements like temperature, light, humidity, and more. AI then applies intricate algorithms to assemble data from sensors, translating them into suitable actions that replicate the pets' native habitats. This automated adjustment procedure, without the owner's constant observation and intervention, ensures a stress-free maintenance routine.

Smart habitat applications are pushing boundaries, aiming to create more robust simulations. Work is being done to incorporate sounds and naturalistic stimuli that exotic pets may encounter in the wild. This implementation of advanced AI functionality would provide a more holistic and natural living space for exotic pets.

10.2. Dietary Management

Another crucial component in exotic pet care that AI is transforming is diet regulation. Exotic pets have very particular dietary requirements to meet their nutritional needs, which can be complex and unique. Automated feeders equip pet owners with a systematic dietary schedule. These smart devices, driven by AI algorithms, adapt according to the pet's eating patterns, ensuring regular and precise meal portions, and reducing the risk of overfeeding or malnutrition.

Moreover, AI technology is being used to develop nutrition profiles for exotic pets. This includes their specific caloric intake, based on species, weight, age, and other factors. This research, propelled by machine learning, would allow owners to tailor diets to their pets' unique needs more accurately and conveniently.

10.3. Health Monitoring Systems

AI systems are facilitating exotic pet owners with proactive health monitoring and early anomaly detection, reducing the implications of unanticipated health issues. Existing devices range from simple tracking of physical activities to advanced biometric data analysis. For example, wearable devices for reptiles analyze their movement patterns, detecting any unusual behavior that could suggest a health problem.

In addition to physical health, the emotional well-being of pets is equally important. Advanced AI systems are achieving this through behavioral analysis algorithms. They track the pet's habits, feeding patterns, activity cycles, and more, identifying any deviations which could indicate stress or discomfort.

10.4. AI Applications in Exotic Pet Training

Training exotic pets is no less than an uphill battle. Here too, AI can lend a helping hand. With continuous reinforcement learning, AI technology can understand and interpret the behavior of the pet, providing owners with insights on their pet's cognitive abilities and personality traits.

Machine learning applications can also make training routines interactive and productive. By understanding the species-specific responses and correlating it with reward-based learning, these methodologies can assist pet owners in effectively reinforcing positive behavior.

10.5. Ethical Concerns and Regulatory Matters

While AI applications promise a revolution in exotic pet care, they also pose a host of ethical and regulatory concerns. Issues range from potential privacy invasions through constant monitoring, implications of overly autonomous systems, to affecting the pet's mental well-being.

Regulatory bodies are already dealing with these concerns to an extent, working to create a balance between technological advancement and ethical implications. This is crucial in ensuring that AI in pet care becomes a tool of empowerment rather than a source of apprehension.

In conclusion, we are at the dawn of the exciting conflux of AI and exotic pet care. As we traverse deeper into this space, we stand to witness the creation of an ecosystem constructed to harmonize the high demands of exotic pet ownership with the convenience of technology – establishing an equilibrium, where artificial intelligence ensures holistic well-being for our unique and cherished companions.

Chapter 11. What's Next? Predicting the Future of AI in Pet Care

As we look ahead, the prospects of using AI in pet care have never seemed brighter and broader. Currently, advancements in AI are revolutionizing many aspects of life, and pet care forms no exception to this trend. The application of machine learning, computer vision, and predictive analytics in pet care is expected to revolutionize the industry, bridging the gap between veterinary care and pet owners, and simplifying tasks ranging from tracking pet health to personalizing pet diets.

11.1. Predictive Analytics, Health Tracking, and AI-Driven Veterinarians

Predictive analytics is leading the charge towards the future, leveraging statistical algorithms and machine-learning techniques to anticipate future outcomes based on historical data. For pet care, smart devices collate information about a pet's activities, movements, and behavior patterns, allowing for analysis and early detection of health problems. In the future, this sort of monitoring and analysis could extend to predict potential ailments or conditions, enabling proactive healthcare actions, ensuring that pets remain healthy and vibrant for as long as possible. The AI-driven predictive model could also suggest personalized dietary adjustments, exercise programs, and sleeping patterns bespoke to each pet's needs.

Additionally, advancements in telemedicine and AI-driven virtual veterinarians are altering how pet health consultations are conducted. The possibility of connecting pet owners to veterinarians through smart devices offers the advantage of receiving medical advice almost instantaneously. Machine learning could also be leveraged to interpret the behavior and health records of pets, providing insight, recommendations and potentially diagnosing conditions without the need for physical examination.

In due course, we may witness a paradigm shift: an AI-driven monitoring system constantly observing pets and communicating with vets. These systems could alert when there is a deviation from the pet's normal state, even before the pet shows noticeable signs of discomfort, allowing for early medical intervention.

11.2. AI and Nutrition Management

The future of AI in pet care also lies in personalizing nutrition for each pet. The next-gen smart feeders are expected to monitor and manage pets' nutrition intake. These devices may be able to identify specific needs of each pet by analyzing micro-nutritional requirements and caloric intake. The data, processed by AI, can allow pet owners to understand the accurate amount of specific nutrients needed by their pets.

Furthermore, machine learning can bring innovation to automatically adjust a pet's dietary needs based on age, weight, activity levels, and overall health. This could result in smart feeders dispensing optimal food quantities, minimizing overfeeding and ensuring that pets maintain a balanced nourishment level.

11.3. Computer Vision for Behavior Analysis

Computer vision, another find in the AI toolbox, is envisaged to play a leading role in behavior analysis. High-resolution cameras paired with intelligent software can monitor pets, identify abnormal behaviors, and alert pet owners in real-time. For example, if a reticent cat suddenly starts pacing restlessly, the system can detect the erratic movement, analyze the deviation, and notify the pet owner about the possible distress signs.

This system can also help in training pets by analyzing their responses to various stimulations and using reinforcement learning to guide the training process. Moreover, computer vision, integrated with image recognition, can help lost pets find their way home. This kind of AI application can recognize pets from images and match them with lost pet databases, helping to reunite lost pets with their worried owners.

11.4. Automated and Enhanced Training through AI

The future might also see an enhanced AI role in designing customized training programs for pets. By monitoring and observing daily actions and habits, AI-enabled devices could evaluate training methodologies suitable for each pet, proposing personalized schedules and strategies. Future AI technology could learn pets' preferences, moods, and temperaments, optimizing training results effectively.

Making pet ownership an easier and rewarding task, automated gadgets, robotics, and AI-controlled wearable tech may redefine discipline, control, and training methods. For instance, a wearable device could track a pet's location and movements, using AI to analyze patterns, familiarize with regular routes, and predict the pet's movements. This can immensely help prevent pets from straying, ultimately reinforcing pet safety.

11.5. Robotics and AI Interaction

Advancements in robotics and AI interaction are also expected to enrich future pet care. Robotic pet companions can interact with pets, providing them with entertainment, mental stimulation, and even physical exercise while the owner is away. These devices could also assess a pet's mood and temperament to adapt the interactive plan to avoid over-stimulating or causing distress.

Looking to the future, we see a large potential for the integration of AI in pet care. Whether it is identifying health issues before they become problematic, facilitating nutrition management, or enhancing training methods, these advancements are poised to help pet owners better understand and care for their pets. They promise a future where pets live longer, healthier, and happier lives.

While these predictions are optimistic, it is also important to understand the ethical implications and responsibility that comes with integrating AI and technology into pet care. As AI continues to grow and intersect with pet care, its responsible use should always be prioritized, ensuring that technology not merely enhances but respects the unique and treasured bond that exists between humans and their pets.

So, as we embrace the dawn of a new era in pet care, enriched by technology, let's remember that at the heart of it all should be the welfare, thriving, and happiness of our beloved pets. Companionship, love, and empathy should never be replaced but only amplified by technology. AI, in the hands of responsible pet owners, can make this amplification possible, leading to a future resplendent in happier tails and contented purrs.